ORANGUTANS

A TRUE BOOK

by

Patricia A. Fink Martin

Children's Press®

A Division of Grolier Publishing

New York London Hong Kong Sydney
Danbury, Connecticut

An orangutan
hangs from a tree.

Reading Consultant
Linda Cornwell
*Coordinator of School Quality
and Professional Improvement
Indiana State Teachers Association*

Content Consultant
Kathy Carlstead, Ph.D.
*National Zoological Park
Washington, D.C.*

The photograph on the cover shows a female orangutan eating leaves. The photograph on the title page shows a male orangutan showing his teeth to scare off another orangutan.

Visit Children's Press® on the Internet at:
http://publishing.grolier.com

Library of Congress Cataloging-in-Publication Data

Martin, Patricia A. Fink, 1955–
    Orangutan / by Patricia A. Fink Martin.
        p. cm. — (A true book)
    Includes bibliographical references and index.
    Summary: Describes the habitat, life cycle, physical characteristics, and behavior of the orangutan.
    ISBN: 0-516-21571-X (lib. bdg.)   0-516-27020-6 (pbk.)
    1. Orangutan—Juvenile literature. [1. Orangutan.] I. Title. II. Series.
QL737.P96M376   2000
599.88'3—dc21
                                                                99-17065
                                                                CIP
                                                                AC

Contents

An orangutan waking up

The Red Ape

As day begins, a big, red-haired animal sits up in its treetop bed of leaves and twigs. It stretches and looks around. The animal's face looks almost human, and so does its body.

The animal is an orangutan. Orangutans live in the tropical

rain forest. Shaggy red hair covers their bodies. You might think these animals are monkeys, but they are not. Monkeys are smaller, and most monkeys have tails.

Orangutans belong to a group of animals called the

great apes. Great apes are larger than monkeys and have no tail. Gorillas, bonobos, and chimpanzees are also great apes. Because orangutans have red fur, they are sometimes called red apes.

A gorilla (left) and a chimpanzee (right) are great apes too.

Orangutans can use their hands and feet to hold onto vines and tree branches.

Scientists place monkeys, apes, and humans into a group of mammals called primates. Primates are smart animals with hands and feet built for grasping. They can use their fingers and toes to pick up and hold objects. Most primates have eyes that face forward, so they can tell whether the objects they see are nearby or far away.

An orangutan's eyes are on the front of its head—just like ours.

Orangutans spend most of their time in trees.

Orangutans are the largest primates that spend time in the rain forest treetops. They live in Southeast Asia, on the islands of Borneo and Sumatra. Smaller apes live there too, but the orangutan is the only great ape to live outside of Africa.

Home in the Rain Forest

The rain forest is very different from other forests you may have visited. The weather in a rain forest is always hot and steamy. It is hottest in the afternoon. In a rain forest, it can rain for several hours each day.

Plants grow everywhere in a rain forest. Huge trees tower above the forest floor. Some vines grow as thick as your leg. They wrap around tree trunks and reach to the sky. Smaller trees and bushes grow beneath the larger trees. Fallen logs and ferns cover the ground. This forest is a giant tangle of stems, leaves, and trunks.

This orangutan swings through the thick tropical rain forest of Sumatra.

Travel in the Treetops

There are so many plants in a rain forest that it is hard to walk through it. This is not a problem for orangutans. They travel through the rain forest by climbing and swinging from tree to tree.

The body of an orangutan is built to hang and swing. Its

An orangutans arms are much longer than its legs.

arms are about twice as long as its legs. They can reach almost 8 feet (2.4 meters) from fingertip to fingertip. When an orangutan lets its arms fall to its sides, they almost reach its ankles.

How far do your arms stretch? Raise your arms to shoulder level, and ask a friend to measure the distance. Now stand up straight. Let your arms hang by your sides. How far down do they reach?

Do your arms stretch as far as an orangutan's?

An orangutan's hands and feet are designed to help it grab and hold onto tree branches.

An orangutan's feet and hands are curved. This helps the animal hold onto tree branches. Its feet look a lot like its hands. An orangutan can grab a branch with its feet or with its hands.

An orangutan moves through the forest by reaching and grabbing vines and branches. But sometimes the trees are not so close together. To reach across a gap, the

A young orangutan looks for a way to cross a gap between two trees.

orangutan finds a springy tree branch and holds on tight with its hands and feet. Then the animal throws its weight from side to side, making the branch bend. The orangutan and the branch sway back and forth together, and the branch bends a little more each time. Soon, the branch reaches all the way across the gap. The orangutan reaches out and grabs the closest leafy branch.

A mother orangutan makes a bridge out of her body so that her baby can move from tree to tree.

When a young orangutan needs help in the treetops, its mother makes a bridge of her body. The little one then crawls across.

Old males are never seen high in the trees. The lighter

Many male orang-utans are too heavy to swing through the trees. They must walk along the ground.

branches up there cannot support their weight. Most females weigh 80 to 100 pounds (36 to 45 kilograms). Male orangutans may weigh up to twice as much, so they must walk on all fours on the forest floor.

How Orangutans Eat

When orangutans are not sleeping or moving, they are eating. The red ape loves fruits. There are many kinds of fruits in the rain forest. Can you find figs, mangoes, or plums in your grocery store? Try one! Orangutans eat these too.

This young orangutan is eating a banana.

This orangutan has picked a bunch of bananas and taken it to the ground.

When an orangutan finds a tree with fruit, the animal eats and eats. Shells and seeds drop to the ground. When all the fruit is eaten, the orangutan leaves to look for more.

Orangutans eat a lot of fruit between April and November. They need to build up a layer of extra fat to help them through the rest of the year. From December to March, many rain forest trees do not bear fruit. Then, the apes feed on bark, leaves, and insects.

This orangutan is using a stick to scoop ants out of a hole in a tree.

Living Alone

An adult red ape spends most of its life alone. Males and females come together to mate. They may stay together for a few days, or even a few weeks. After that, they separate. Male orangutans always avoid each other. Each day, a male travels a few miles looking for food. He may meet other orangutans, but he almost never meets another adult male.

Adult males keep track of each other by calling. At least once a day, each male performs a special ritual. He begins by breaking a tree branch and slamming it to the ground. He may push over a dead tree. Then he lets out a long call using a special pouch in his throat.

A male orangutan uses a special pouch in his throat to make a loud call.

Next a terrifying roar is heard through the forest. Louder and louder he roars. Finally, the roar turns into a bubbling gurgle and fades away. A male's call can be heard more than 1 mile (1.6 kilometers) away.

Female orangutans spend some time living with their young. A newborn orangutan clings tightly to its mother. For almost a year, a mother orangutan holds her baby

A baby orangutan clings tightly to its mother.

Young orangutans often spend some time alone, but their mother is never too far away.

close all the time. The young orangutan drinks milk, but eats no solid food.

The young ape will soon leave its mother's side. But the mother is always nearby. Young orangutans like to play. They climb trees and vines. While a mother orangutan naps, her little one swings from a tree branch. It practices building a nest and draping leaves over its head.

This young orangutan is munching on some leaves.

Growing Up

When an orangutan is 3 or 4 years old, it stops drinking its mother's milk. It may also stop sleeping in its mother's nest. The young orangutan spends its days searching for food or other orangutans to play with. At night, it goes back to its mother.

These young orangutans are playing on a vine.

When an orangutan is 8 or 9 years old, it leaves its mother for good. When it meets other orangutans its own age, the youngsters stay together for a time, playing and eating.

Females are full grown by age 10, but some have their first baby when they are as young as 7 years old. Males take longer to grow up. They may not be full grown until they are 15 years old.

The orangutan is an endangered species.

Endangered Species

No one knows how many orangutans are left in the wild. There may be fewer than 20,000. At one time, the red ape lived in what are now the country of China and the island of Java. But now there are no orangutans left in these places.

This zookeeper is caring for a baby orangutan.

Someday the orangutan may become extinct. It is now an endangered species. Even though it is against the law to kill an orangutan, some people still hunt them. When these poachers kill a mother orang-utan, they often capture her young and sell them to zoos or circuses. They even sell some to people who keep the orangutans as pets.

The places where orang-utans live are also in danger.

Their rain forest homes are being cut down. The trees are used to make buildings and the cleared land is used for farming and raising cattle. As tropical rain forests grow smaller and smaller, the animals get crowded. It is hard for them to find food.

You can help the orangutans. Read other books about these animals. Learn about the rain forest. Recycle paper and newspaper. This

Not long ago, the area where this boy is standing was a lush tropical rain forest.

These orangutans are eating at a feeding station built by scientists.

means that fewer trees are cut down for wood. Tell other people what you have learned. Join a club that aids endangered animals. Help raise money for their projects. Support an orphaned orangutan baby through the Orangutan Foster Parent Program.

You do not have to do all of these things. Even one action can help. Together, we can save these gentle red apes.

To Find Out More

If you would like to learn more about orangutans and their rain forest home, check out these additional resources.

 **Books**

Cherry, Lynne. **First Wonders of Nature: Orangutan.** Dutton Children's Books, 1998.

Darling, Tara and Kathy Darling. **How to Babysit an Orangutan.** Walker and Company, 1996.

Gallardo, Evelyn. **Among the Orangutans: The Biruté Galdikas Story.** Chronicle Books, 1993.

Horton, Casey. **Apes.** Benchmark Books, 1996.

Maynard, Thane. **Primates: Apes, Monkeys and Prosimians.** Franklin Watts, 1994.

Woods, Mae. **Orangutans.** Abdo & Daughters, 1998.

💡 Organizations and Online Sites

The Orangutan Foundation International (OFI)
Orangutan Foster Parent Program
822 South Wellesley Avenue
Los Angelos, CA 90049
http://www.ns.net/ orangutan

International Primate Protection League
P.O. Box 766
Summerville, SC 29484
http://www.ippl.org

The Nature Conservancy Adopt-an-Acre Program
1815 North Lynn Street
Arlington, VA 22209

Orangutan Facts
http://www.ns.net/ orangutan/facts.html

The site features photos and information about orangutans and has a map that shows where they live.

Rainforest Action Network
221 Pine Street, Suite 500
San Francisco, CA 94104
http://www.ran.org/kids _action/index.html

Important Words

endangered species a kind of living thing that is in danger of dying out

extinct no longer existing on Earth

great ape the largest of the apes, this group includes the orangutan, the gorilla, the chimpanzee, and the bonobo

mammal a type of vertebrate (an animal with a backbone) that is covered with hair, is warm-blooded, and produces milk for its young

poacher someone who kills or captures wild animals illegally

primate a mammal with a large brain and grasping hands

ritual a series of actions that is repeated on a regular basis

Index

Meet the Author

Patricia A. Fink Martin has a doctorate in biology. After working in the laboratory and teaching for 10 years, she began writing science books for children. *Booklist* chose her first book, *Animals that Walk on Water*, as one of the ten best animal books for children in 1998. Dr. Martin lives in Tennessee with her husband, Jerry, and their daughter, Leslie.

Photographs ©: ENP Images: 7 right, 8, 12, 19, 22, 23, 30, 32, 34, 42 (Gerry Ellis); Fundamental Photos: 15 (Richard Megna); National Geographic Image Collection: 4 (Timothy Laman), 10 (Michael K. Nichols); Photo Researchers: 9 (Toni Angermayer), 6, 16, 17, 24, 29 (Tim Davis), 38 (Dan Guravich), 11 (Jacques Jangoux), 41 (Wayne Lawler), 1, 2, 14, 20, 36 (Renee Lynn), cover (Tom McHugh), 7 left (OKAPIA); Visuals Unlimited: 27 (Leonard Lee Rue III).

Read these other
TRUE BOOKS
about primates

Chimpanzees

Gorillas

Lemurs, Lorises,
and Other Lower Primates

Monkeys of Asia and Africa

Monkeys of Central
and South America

CHILDREN'S PRESS

U.S. $6.95
Can. $9.95